Encouragement & Loving Admonishings

Encouragement and loving admonishings

to help us through our journeys

By Marie Miller

Library and Archives Canada Cataloguing in Publication

Miller, Marie, 1954-
    Encouragement and loving admonishings / Marie Miller.

Poems.
ISBN 978-1-896213-58-3

    I. Title.

PS8626.I4521E63 2010   C811'.6   C2010-900059-5

Copyright © 2010 Marie Miller

All rights reserved.

Published in Canada by:
byDesign Media
12730 Simcoe Street, Port Perry L9L 1B3
E-mail diane@bydesignmedia.ca
www.bydesignmedia.ca
Layout and Design: Diane Roblin-Lee

No part of this publication may be reproduced, stored in a retrieval system, or transmitted in any form or by any means without prior permission of the copyright owner.

Dedication

I would like to dedicate these poems to my loving son and to my friend and sister, Nicole, in thanks for their prayers and love, and for giving me the determination to pursue publishing them. And most of all to God, who gave me this gift to share, to encourage both others and myself to follow Him. I want to give the honor and glory to Jesus my Lord and Saviour.

Contents

My Biography 7
My Journey 9
My Mother & Dad 10
God's Peace 16
A Prayer 17
A Soldier Of Jesus 18
Are You Saved? 19
Bad Habits 21
Bless Our Family ~ a Song 24
Caring 25
Change is the Key 26
Day and Night We Give You Thanks 28
Desires Of Lusts 30
Different People 32
Fighting 33
Freedom Forever 35
Salt to the Earth 36
God Almighty 37
God Covered Me 39
God is Calling You 40
God's Promise 41

His Vessels	42
I Believe In God	43
I'll Tell You ~ a Song	44
I'm Not Ashamed of Jesus' Name	46
Jesus is our Salvation	47
Jesus our Anchor	48
More of You ~ a Prayer	49
My Promise to You	50
Obedience is Worship	51
Our Times are in His Hands	52
Scriptures that Encourage My Heart	53
Seek, Thirst and Love	54
Storms I Go Through	55
Strength for Your Journey	56
Temptation	57
Thank You	58
The Wrong Way	60
This Old World	62
This Season	64
The Great I Am	65
We Are Traveling Pilgrims	66
We Need Sanctification	67
Your Love In Me	69

My Biography
Marie Miller

I was born on June 18th, 1954, at Toronto General Hospital and was cyanotic (a blue baby). I had to go to Sick Kids' Hospital until I was well. When I did leave, I was put into a foster home as my mother could not look after me. She was too young and so decided to put me up for adoption – but I never did get adopted. I went to three other foster homes and finally got to stay in the last one until I got married. To me, these are my loving parents. I have a sister and two brothers. Even though my birth mother had to give me up and my dad was not involved, I still love them no matter what. I hope they are okay and happy and most of all I hope they have given their lives to the Lord.

I have been married for 34 years and have a son who now has a family of his own. There have been many challenges, but I have gotten through them with the Lord's help and am still being challenged to grow more. My son and his wife are both born-again Christians and I thank the Lord that they are. They are all a blessing and very precious to my husband and me. Oshawa, Ontario has been my home for the last 19 years.

I have been writing poems since I gave my life to the Lord and have been wondering if this is my gift or whether it is something else, but I now know that this is it. I enjoy writing and sharing the truth. Sometimes I am not sure of some of the words and feel uncomfortable, but I realize that it is not about comfort, but about what we need to hear. I believe that my Heavenly Father has revealed to me what you and I both need to know, through the writing of my poems.

I pray that these words will continue to encourage and bless you in your walk with the Lord. I am still learning, trusting, waiting and trying to be obedient. God's Word both calms and convicts us and seems to jump out at us when we need it. When I need him the most, He is ready to hear me. He has gotten me through many challenges and I give him thanks for each day. He is my all in all and my provider. He is a wonderful Saviour to us, don't you think?

One of my favorite scriptures is Proverbs 3:5-6, *"Trust in the Lord with all your heart, and lean not on your own understanding; in all your ways acknowledge Him, and He will direct your paths."*

And also Isaiah 40:31, *"But they that wait upon the Lord will renew their strength, they will mount up with wings as eagles, they shall run and not be weary, they shall walk and not faint."*

May we always read and do what He says in His Word, especially show his love. God bless you all. Remember to keep on looking up; this may be the day that we will meet Him in the air.

My Journey

My journey is like puzzle pieces
that link together
each minute of the day.
There is a reason for all of this.
God has planned them in His own way.

But thoughts keep rolling in my mind
about what He's up to.
But when I think of all the amazing
things He has done, I don't have to worry.
It's His will that will be done!

My Mother & Dad

Not knowing my birth mother and dad is very, very hard.

I hope that one day I will see them in Heaven.

Most days I think about them and what
we could have done when I was just a wee one.

We could have gone to the zoo,
or even to the park,
riding on the teeter-totter, just us three.

We could have gone on the swings
and slid on the slide together.

When we got home I could have watched TV
as Mom would make dinner for Daddy and me.
Then she would have read a book or I could
have read to her and after a long and tiring day,
she would bathe me.

"Good night," she would have said, "I love you,"
and put me to bed.

And even on days when she would walk
me to school,
she would have held my hand and talked with me.
At times I would probably have talked too much,
but she would have always been smiling.
And then she would have given me a hug and a kiss
and said, "Have a good day. I'm going to miss you."

And when it was time for my teen-age years, I would
have dressed in nifty clothes and done my hair all
different ways to look real nice for the boys.
She would have told me all I had to know about the
things to do and the things not to do so I
would not get hurt.
I would probably not have always listened, but I would
have tried to remember her words.

I would have gone to high-school with some of my
friends and gotten to know a few new ones too.
I hope she would have taken me to

church to learn of God's truth in the Bible.
We would have sung and clapped to the wonderful hymns
and gotten to know Jesus and how He loves us.

Then as I grew I would have become a young lady,
mature in every way, but still always learning.
I would have maybe gone to go to a college and majored
in something I like to do to further my education.
And when I would have finished all of that, I would have
been able to get a job, and an apartment too.

Maybe I'd have worked to help little children, or written
poems to publish and have my own book.
I would hope she would be very proud of me,
and love me no matter what I thought of doing.

And then one day I would meet young men,
hoping they would treat me nice.
They would take me to dances and I would talk with
them and say I love you, and things like that.

I'd remember all the things she told me, because
if I didn't, I know she might be upset
and sad, but she would get over it and say
"I still love you."

Time would pass and I would meet a man –
kind, loving and handsome,
who would love me for who I am, not only
because he had to.
We would get engaged and plan our wedding.
She would help us out because that's what moms
and dads do to get things ready.
Many months would all go by and soon
the time would come
and my husband-to-be would be standing
there waiting for me, probably not patiently,
but still, waiting for his bride-to-be.
I would be with her for this last time as she fixes
my dress and headpiece and says, "I'm so proud
of you, but don't forget all the things I said," and
kisses me on the forehead.

Now it is time to leave her and walk down the aisle
to meet the handsome man I am going to marry.
The day has come and I would say, "I'm getting
ready to meet my husband."

There's a knock at the door; it's the camera man.
He's come to take some pictures.
Then it's off to the church and up the stairs as I wait
for the music.
The wedding guests are waiting as the bridal party
walks through.
Then it's my turn to walk the aisle, as the guests
begin to stand,
with heads turning and cameras flashing
and I walk towards my future husband.

He looks at me and I look at him and we give each
other a smile.
Dad places my hand in his and says, "It's time."
When the pastor asks, "Who's giving her away?"
Dad says, "It is I," and goes to sit beside his wife.

Pastor prays for us as we all bow our heads. Then
after that we say our vows and kiss each other
as the pastor says
we are one. "This is now Mr. and Mrs."

As we walk back down the aisle, I turn. As I look
back, they wave and give me a smile
and I think ~ that's my mom and dad!

God's Peace

My peace is like a river flowing within you,
casting those dark shadows away.
My love is like an ocean pouring over you,
casting all your burdens away.
My hope is like a garden where flowers
bloom everywhere,
and My salvation is like a hiding place
where you and I can share.

There are habits I want to take from you
that are not who you are,
and if you let me have them, you will go far.
I'll make you into the person I want you to be.
I am your Heavenly Father.

A Prayer

Lord thank you for this time
I get to spend with You,
for learning all I can.
You show that you care and teach me
how to be kind to someone in this world.

I can open my heart to someone who
needs a shoulder,
to share a piece of bread, or give
some laughs to take away the fear.

Continue to show me Lord,
how I can get closer to someone
who is lost,
So I can let them know that You love them.

A Soldier Of Jesus

Will I be soldier in His army?

Will I go forth with strength?

Can I be listener and doer

amid all the heart-aches?

Can I stand up for what is right,

always pressing on;

or will I wait until someone else

is bold enough to step out in

my place?

Are You Saved?

"Are you saved?" asked the preacher;
"Do you really know Him?"
I listened to the words he spoke
and had to think about it once more.
He asked some questions about what
I'm doing and if I really know Him
~ the Lord.

I realized that even though I'd said
the "sinners prayer" those many
years ago,
I'd thought I could live like the devil
~ but it wasn't so.

He asked me if I am continuing in Him
and in His Word, growing and serving,
proving to be His disciple,
and if He is the purpose for my life, itself.

Is He *your* salvation? Do people see a
change in *you*?
Or do you keep on sinning when Jesus says,
"Sin no more."
Are you the same person who you
used to be?

Are you excited to want to know and
be like Him,
to let your light so shine that people will
see your works, and glorify His Name?

Do they see His love in you? Are you more
confident in Him and not in yourself, humble,
having more of a heart
for people, and for your brethren, than you
used to have?
If so, you *are* His disciple and you know
you *are* saved.
And now that you know, let's share the truth.

Bad Habits

When people talk, do they listen
to themselves?
Or do they keep prattling on,
forgetting, and thinking that they
are the boss?
Do they do the things they want to do
because it makes them feel better?
They just don't have any idea or respect
for us, those weaker than another.

No matter what we say or do, it seems
they do not care.
How much more do we have to
put up with this? I know You said,
"Seventy times seven."

We know it's up to You Lord, but we
don't know how much of this
we can take.

It seems they don't have You on their minds.
We're sorry if we're telling You how to do it;
we know we don't have the right ~
but we are asking You Lord. We really need
Your help. It is killing us inside.

So please Lord, won't you help them to
get control of these bad habits that kill,
so we can have a cleaner home and start
to do things together again.

I know they don't want us to nag. They say
one day they will stop,
but don't they know that they cannot do it
without Your help?
Don't they want to be free of these anxieties?

In Your Word it says that pride comes before
the fall. That's what the devil did.

He fell at the start because he wanted
to be called God.

If only they would give in and let You,
Lord, bring them out.
What a difference that would make.
And when they understand Your truth,
I hope they'll praise Your Name,
and let the world really know who's Boss ~
The Lord God!

Isaiah 32:17

Bless Our Family
(A Song)

Bless our family, Lord we pray.

Thanks for keeping us safe today.

Help to show us right from wrong.

When we're weak you'll keep us strong.

Work on our characters too.

Help us grow in our walk with You.

And our gifts, give us to use.

Let them honor and glorify You.

Caring

What's happening to the children?

Don't people care anymore?

So much shooting, trafficking and hunger.

How much more will this go on?

I remember when children played outside.

We didn't have much, but we survived.

Each morning at school we would say the

Lord's prayer,

but now they have taken it out of there.

Don't they know it is better to fight for what's right

than to fight for what's evil?

So many of our children are hurting ~ they are crying inside

for someone to love them. People must put themselves aside.

Concentrate on someone else who might need their love.

Can we, each of us, just reach one at a time?
~ hear their cry?

Change Is The Key

Change is the key if you want to grow.
"Are you willing?" asks God,
"Just let me know.
Will you allow Me to do what needs to be done ~
or will you harden your hearts and close your ears?
It's not so much of what you want, but more of Me. I've got a lot to give.

Life without My truth is not life at all.
You need it to sustain yourself in this mixed-up world.
So if you want this change it has to be your choice.
It's not only for unbelievers, but for those who are following faithfully too.

Your have but today that I shall give

for you don't know about tomorrow until

that day,

so use it wisely in Jesus' Name.

Day And Night We Give You Thanks

Whistling winds and

gusting waves on the seashore.

The moon rises up to give its light

stars twinkle ~ each one so bright.

The sun sets down for a rest...

colours of the sky so perfect

oranges, reds and yellows.

As a new day appears,

beams of light break open wide

through the clouds to see a new day.

Give thanks to the Lord,

for one more dawn.

Crisp winter nights of

soft feathered flakes of snow~

each a different, patterned shape

falling gracefully to the ground.

God's best is magnificent.

His beauty surrounds the earth

and even the fragrance of each flower

has it own unique zest.

Desires Of Lusts

All the time we need your help Lord,

with the fruit of self-control,

for there are many things we want

to explore.

One may be the love of money ~ when

we don't have much we are not content

and want more.

And other desires that we can't mention ~ but

You know.

When we yield to these desires of lust

we open a door,

to allow Satan and his subtle craftiness entice

us even more.

And he says, "I got you ~ you'll never get out of

this one

and we think we never will.

'Cause he works in how we speak out

and makes us think this will help us

or is good.

He's very clever, and deceitful.

But God our Father has given us the whole

armour of God,

that we may be able to stand in these

evil days and overcome them all.

We have God's truth, righteousness, peace and

faith, so that we can extinguish all the fiery darts

of the wicked one.

The helmet of salvation and the sword of the Spirit, which is

the Word of God. I believe it is the strongest.

And that is enough to hold us because of His

strength and love.

Psalms 63:8 119:65-72

1 Timothy 6:10

Ephesians 6:11-18

Different People

Where is the love that we once had?
Did we forget where it came from?
What have we shown to those
you gave us, Lord?
Did we show them how we care?

Do we give them compassion
or do we look the other way?
Are we not supposed to be your ambassadors ~
people different from the world?

Do we not remember that
we have to come before you and
give an account of what we did?

Help us, oh Lord, to think
not only of ourselves, but of others too
and to remember it's not about us;
it's about what You have been doing.

Fighting

So many parents in Israel and Palestine
are teaching their children how to fight.
They pack them up with bombs because
they think this is right.

They say they are doing this to please
their god,
but this is not the same God that I know
about.
"Vengeance is mine," God says, "not this way
do I fight."
My God must not only be angry, but sad at
this plight.

These little children should be playing,
full of laughter and of joy ~
but all they know how to do is hate the
people in this world.

This should be a time of loving others
as they would want to be loved,
but how can people know this, if their
parents are not telling them.

From generation to generation it has
gone too far.
Now their children will teach their children
to make war.

They have to want to change if they
want love for themselves,
and only one person can change them.
His name is Jesus Christ.
He came to save the world.

Freedom Forever

There maybe nothing free in this world
or even lasting,
but if you have Jesus Christ, you have freedom
forever.

You may be lonely because of what people do
or say,
but remember ~ you can't be lonely with Jesus
in any way.

He will show you what you need to learn from
His Book,
He will always love and care for you no matter
how things look.

So trust Him in every circumstance, and rest upon
His Word.
Don't think that you know what to do on your own,
for one slip and you can get hurt.
The only way that you can be free is to seek Him first.

Salt to the Earth

We must be salt to the earth

to those who don't have much hope,

showing Christ in us, for He is the light of the world.

Comforting, not condemning, remembering that

we were once there.

Soothing the wounds of others, not giving more pain,

delighting to help them in any way we can with our time

and our love,

telling them that whatever trials they have to go through

can be lifted up to the Lord if they're willing to pray.

But most of all share our faith and hope in the one

and only God,

not only in many words, but simply, like a child.

God Almighty

There are many people who put their
faith in other men,
instead of in the One who can give them
new life.
"Who is He?" you ask. Jesus the Son
of God.

Not Mohammed, nor Buddha, not Allah;
not even new-agers who say they are gods
~ a thought Satan put in their heads.
He's such a liar. He never speaks the truth.

There's only one God Almighty who made
the heavens and earth,
and from the beginning He not only did it
for Himself, but for us who He made.

Too many people think they're going to heaven by doing good deeds, but that's not what the Lord says in my Bible.

Take a look inside and see for yourself the treasures of this Book. You will be surprised at what you find; it's worth more than gold.
Psalms 96:4

God Covered Me

God covered me with His love, His love ~

A tender moment, a whisper of truth.

He wrapped me up so abundantly in His arms

that in my heart I could feel His presence of peace.

A time to cherish His hope in faith, and nothing

can diminish His love for me.

God is Calling You

God is calling you to come to be with Him.

Why don't you want to hear?

You know your life is getting worse

and you are feeling very weary.

You may not have another day

to hear His Holy Spirit call you.

Won't you just give Him a chance

to get to know you?

You'll be surprised to find how much

He really, really loves you.

God's Promise

Jesus loves you no matter
what you've done.
Don't you want to know Him?
He is God's only Son.

His love for you is everlasting.
No one else can give you that
kind of love.
He is waiting for you to come.
He will never leave you alone.
Please, don't think you can do
it on your own;
you can't. You need to surrender.

Life will not always be easy.
But afflictions will be just for
a moment.
He will get you through them,
by whatever He lays on your heart.

2 Corinthians 4:17

His Vessels

If we lose our eyes, we still have our

voices to speak.

If we lose our voices, we still have our hands

to hold out and embrace.

If we lose our hands we still have our feet

to take a step of faith.

If we lose our feet we still have our minds to pray.

If we lose our minds, God can heal us through His

own will and way in Jesus Name.

So we can't say we don't have ways of serving

Him,

no matter our defeat.

God made us His vessels to do what we can

by giving what we have to give.

I Believe In God

I believe in God, but it's more than that.
He is my Savior, Lord and Heavenly Father.
I have this personal relationship
that no matter where I am in this life,
I can talk with Him.

Whatever my problems are,
my Jesus will never leave me.
He will always be near.

He loves everyone so much,
whether black, white, or pale.
And if you get know Him,
you can call Him *your* Heavenly Father.
as well.

I'll Tell You
(A Song)

Too many things we keep inside us

that we don't want others to hear ~

but Satan cheers.

We open a door so he can depress us,

thinking we can't get out of our mess.

Don't we know we have the authority

to break those chains that hold us,

and stamp out worry and fear in Jesus Name?

The devil gets very angry when he doesn't

get his way,

but we are our Father's heirs and we have victory

over him.

So let's take the time to pray and know that Jesus

has control.

Refrain:

I'll tell you that He loves you.

I'll tell you that He cares.

Just let Him put His arms around you

He will keep you there.

I'm Not Ashamed of Jesus' Name

I'm not ashamed of Jesus' Name.

I'll lift Him up, 'cause He's still the same.

He stands beside me when things are tough.

No matter what, I keep pressing on ~

even when it hurts.

With His strength I will be strong.

I want to live for Him only.

Hallelujah, for He's my Savior and King!

I give Him all the glory.

Jesus is our Salvation

Salvation is a gift from God that's very special,
for through His Son Jesus, He came to save us ~
not through what we do, lest we boast, because
it will not get us into heaven
unless we believe in His only Son.
He says, "I am the way the truth and the life.
No one comes to the Father except through Me."

He wants you to know Him as Prince
of Peace, King of kings, Lord of lords
and Almighty God, our Saviour.
He loves you so, and He wants you to know
that your life with Him will be different.

Following Him won't be easy
but this path you must take,
for only He knows what is best for you
so trust Him, in Jesus' Name.

Jesus our Anchor

Sometimes our storms get stronger.
The waves seem so high that we can't touch them
and we don't know what's going on.
But we have an anchor that holds fast to secure us;
His Name is Jesus and He's waiting for you to
come aboard.

He will flush out our fears to get us through
our trials
and sorrows;
to give us strength when there's no other way to
receive it.
Cry out to Him, the one and only
Lord and Saviour.
He will hear you.
He's waiting patiently for you.

More Of You
A Prayer

Your peace is like a river freely flowing,
A calm before the storm ~
Everlasting.

You've help me to change in these past
few years,
to be the kind of woman you want
me to be and I thank You.

I know I need more help and guidance
through Your Word and Your Holy Spirit
to better equip me to serve You.

Please give me more of You, precious Jesus.
Continue to fill me up with Your Spirit, O Lord,
so I can know You more and more.

My Promise To You

"Are you following Me?" asked Jesus,
"or just pretending?
Do you obey My words or only
please men?
Are you doubting, or are you trusting
that all things are possible from Me?

"Do you think you can do things
on your own without letting Me help you,
or are you willing to wait till I give you clearance?

"Don't you understand that I love you
and I am going to get you through it?
Everything that comes in your life
will soon pass; it is only temporary.
It is My promise to you."

Obedience Is Worship

As Your children, can't we just trust You?
Is it so hard to do?
If we look in Your Word and look for Your wisdom,
we will find what we need to do.

You didn't say marriage would be easy.
There are bumps in the road and mountains along
the journey.
But if we remember that obedience is worship
we won't have to figure out which way to go.

So let's try to show love to our husbands or wives
in a compassionate way, encouraging and building
each other up.

Showing this troubled world what to do
and how to work it out
as we follow our Lord Jesus Christ.

Our Times Are In His Hands

Our time is in His hands
and we don't know what tomorrow
will bring, for God only gives us today.
A day to get to know each other.

For Jesus gives us a little time
to give each other our love and care,
and to appreciate all the little things
each of us need to share.

For what God gives us is meant to be
very special,
for each moment He watches,
what we will do.

He knows we only have this day
to give what His Son
wants to give us too ~

His love.

For He is in control

and everything happens according to

His will.

Scriptures That Encourage My Heart

Isaiah 40:31　　　　Ephesians 6:11-18

Psalms 27　　　　　Galatians 5

Psalms 37　　　　　Philippians 4:13

Psalms 51　　　　　Colossians 3:23-25

Psalms 121　　　　 1 John 5:18-21

John 3:16-17　　　 John 15

Seek, Thirst and Love

Drink it in, drink it in.

Thirst for the Word from the Lord.

Let it drench and overflow you

like the rain that falls

on each petal of a rose.

Seek to find it, seek to find it.

It's more precious than silver and gold.

Love it, just love it.

It's the only thing in this world

that can quench the thirst in your soul

~ the presence of the Lord.

Storms I Go Through

I often wonder if I didn't have my Lord Jesus,
what would I do?
Who would I run to?
Where would I go?

When I go through storms and I lose my way
there wouldn't be any escape.
But I know I can hold my Father's hand.
He's watching over me every second of the day,

looking to see if I will make the right choice,
willing to trust Him and not doubt.
If the storms come my way ~ and they will ~
He will give me the strength to overcome them.

Strength For Your Journey

When you're feeling lonely
and you need to cry,
remember Who is with you;
then you can start to smile.

Times may be rough
or you may not feel well,
but just remember Jesus.
His love will prevail.

He can be your strong tower
when trials come to you.
He has promised He will be there
if you will just trust Him.

Please don't get discouraged;
it will be okay.
This too will pass because He said so
and there is strength for your journey.

Temptation

If what we say or do is not pleasing
to the Lord, then why do we do it?
Is it because we think it will help us...
or is it because we want to shut God out
and do it on our own.

Our thoughts makes us sink and we get
weak under pressure.
Circumstances come and those things
take over
and we yield to temptation.

But if we let Him, Jesus will take control
and I know He will.
I know that we can do all things through Christ
if we surrender everything to Him
and others can see who we really are ~
conquerors through Christ.
We can do nothing without Him.

Thank You

Thank you Lord
for coming to save me.
Thank you for making
me clean and whole.

Thank you for always being there
to take my burdens, and even for the joys
You give me to share.

Thank you for forgiving me and
helping me to change,
for each day you have given
me Your Grace.

Thank you for giving me Your
love, strength and faith,
and with Your Holy Spirit,
teaching me to be still.

Lifting me up when I might stumble

telling me not to always grumble.

I thank you Lord for letting me know You.

I'm so glad You did.

The Wrong Way

Once you've come to know the Lord
Satan will attack.
If you were to follow him
there'd be destruction from the start.

Don't give in to him when you're
weary and depressed.
It's his way of telling you it's alright.

A deceiver is he, and a liar;
not only sly, but thoughtless too.
You think what you are doing is right,
but, wait ~ it's just the beginning.

Don't you know he's waiting
to overtake your little mind,
and let you think you are a nobody
who's not worthy of Jesus' love.

Darts and arrows he will throw,

thorns will prick, and stones he'll whirl.

He says all you have to do is this ~

bow down and worship him, his

idols and wickedness.

This Old World

I want to get out of this old world.
Don't want it's lifestyle anymore.
I want to be close as I can to you Lord.
I know each day I'm doing better.
The things of this world are getting darker
and the things of heaven are bright.
I know I won't have any regrets.
Just being with You is the best thing ever.

I'm learning each day to abide in You.
Sometimes the things I need to lay down
are hard,
but I know that You will give me the strength
to overcome them.
You said in Your Word not to be afraid but
be strong
Lord Jesus help me to learn from the things
I have done.
Out of them I know You will bless me.

My troubles sometimes seem endless, but I know they're not.

You will get me through them no matter what, and I know I will still praise You.

You are my King forever.

This Season

I am in a new season where I need some

more faith and strength to carry me on.

I want to leave my old ways that have

held me down,

but I can't seem to let go of my past.

I'm trying. I need Your help Lord.

I ask for your wisdom and patience

as I get into Your Word to know Your truth.

I know You love me and

know what's best for me

and what I can do.

The Great I Am

Why is it hard for us to be still,

to listen to God and the words

He wants to tell us?

Why is it hard to understand His ways?

When we are weak,

He'll make us strong.

Our impossibilities are not impossible

with Him, for He is in control

of everything.

Remember who He is, and

who He will always be

~ the great "I Am."

We Are Traveling Pilgrims

We are traveling pilgrims going far and wide,

roaming down in the valleys and up the mountain side.

The mountains seem exhausting,

the valleys overwhelming.

We're not sure of what He is doing,

and it may not be very

exciting now, but He's working it out for our good,

where we can rest and lay our heads.

We can learn from our past. That will help us grow.

He will lead us on to a better life.

We Need Sanctification

Why do people think they can get away
with anything?
Do they think that God is not watching
or do they just not care?
We lie and do other things that don't
please Him
and yet say we are following the Lord ~
when we think we can get away with it.

Don't we remember what God's Word says?
How many times do we read it and only
listen, but not do what He says?
Is it only when we are in church services
that we please Him?
We go to our jobs or schools or other places
and act like fools sometimes and they don't
see any difference in us.

We need to look deep in our lives and characters and be willing to change,

because it's in our hearts where God looks and sees our true selves.

We do need sanctification.

Your Love In Me

Father give me a heart to love people

no matter what they are like,

that they may see Your love in me

and want to know You.

Please give me more compassion and

kindness overflowing.

Mercy and grace You gave to me,

so I need to give them some, too.

Help me to show Your light today

just in case I have only this one chance,

so they can get to know You and

to have Your abundance of joy.

www.ingramcontent.com/pod-product-compliance
Lightning Source LLC
Chambersburg PA
CBHW071033080526
44587CB00015B/2596